Prophetic Encounters

*Facilitating Change
By The Spirit*

Prophetic Encounters

*Facilitating Change
By The Spirit*

Jana Alcorn

PROPHETIC ENCOUNTERS
Facilitating Change By The Spirit

Unless otherwise indicated, all Scripture quotations are taken from the *King James Version* of the Bible (KJV).

Prophetic Encounters:
Facilitating Change By The Spirit

ISBN 978-0-9717543-0-0
Library of Congress Control Number: 2002090198
©2001 Jana Alcorn

For more information, visit www.JanaAlcorn.com

Printed in the United States of America.

All rights reserved under International Copyright Law.
Contents and/or cover may not be reproduced in whole or in part in any form without the express written consent of the Publisher.

CONTENTS

Foreword *9*

Introduction 11

Adhere Strictly To My Spirit 12

I Am Rallying Others 14

Formed For My Glory 16

Stirring You For Change 18

The Current Press 20

Increased Strength 22

You Will Be Brought Forth 24

Purged To Strengthen 26

Set In Order That Which Lacks 28

I Am Not Moved By This Storm 30

Tell Me Of Your Hunger 32

Clothed With Me 34

The Weight Of Your Heart 36

Bring Forth The Acceleration 38

Called To Write 40

Declare What I Have Given 42

Enlargement	44
Release Of Resources	46
Spirit Of Confidence	48
There Must Be A Severing	50
The Reformation	52
Re-Define And Re-Evaluate	54
Beyond The Position Of Predictability	56
You Will Have A Plan	58
I Am Moving You	60
You Are In My Hand	62
I Take Responsibility	64
New Investments	66
New Seasons	68
A Hearing Heart	70
The School Of Humility	72
I Have Already Heard	74
A New Communion	76
Arise In A New Mind	78
Refining Time	80

A Place Of Letting Go 82

Come Before Me And Receive Clarity 84

Let Me Reposition You 86

Changes...NOW! 88

Positioned For Choice 90

Old Methods Will Not Suffice 92

You Are Getting Ready For Change 94

I Am Found In Solitude 96

Qualified For This Will 98

Stand And Tell 100

I Plan Ahead For You 102

Anxious To Move For You 104

I Am Processing You 106

Tune Your Ear To My Spirit 108

Say It Out Loud! 110

Alignment Of Mind And Emotions 112

A New Dimension 114

About The Author 117

Foreword

Dr. Jana Alcorn, a powerful and effective voice for the move of God in our generation, has done something ground breaking in this new devotional. It is a needed first for the new millennium. She has taken the power of prophetic utterance and coupled it with daily meditation on a particular Scripture. Each power encounter highlights an issue of extreme relevance for the last day Church. Jesus was concerned about not merely hearing what He said on the surface of His words, He wanted us to hear the deeper meaning of what He was revealing. So too, as He admonished His disciples, this woman of God admonishes you dear reader. Let those that have ears to hear, listen deeply at the level of significance for which these daily encounters have been designed. Bravo Dr. Alcorn!

Dr. Mark J. Chironna
The Master's Touch International Church
Orlando, Florida

Introduction

God is speaking with great clarity in these last days. He is a speaking God and is making His voice known. May you find a place of confidence as you hear the Word of the Lord to your life in the days to come. A Prophetic Encounter is about to change your season! Be activated by His empowering voice!

Jana Alcorn
www.JanaAlcorn.com

Loving God,
Lifting People,
Launching Destinies

Encounter 1

Adhere Strictly To My Spirit

Proverbs 8:20-21
I lead in the way of righteousness, in the midst of the paths of judgment: That I may cause thee that love me to inherit substance; and I will fill their treasures.

I am ready to lead you, says the Lord. I have been standing by waiting for you to recognize Me. Now that you realize that the flesh does not profit, I am going to cause you to become aware of Me. There is nothing that you can do without Me, says the Lord; for you have tried and you have failed. I have not allowed you to be utterly cast down, for I know that there have been things that you have tried and found wanting. I have given time for these things to prove their futility. Now, I am coming to you again, says the Lord. I will raise you up in My power and I will raise you up in Glory, for what I am about to do will require the strictest of adherence to My Spirit. Do not deviate from what I am doing in this season. I require you to focus. Focus as you have never focused. Focus, says the Lord, for I am going to give you moments in My glory. Focus totally upon Me and you will stand in amazement at what shall be accomplished, says the Lord!

Prayer:

**Lord,
Your glory can raise those who are cast down. Help me to focus on the things upon which Your eyes are fixed.
In Jesus' Name,
Amen**

Personal Check Points:

_____
_____
_____
_____
_____
_____
_____

Encounter 2

I Am Rallying Others

John 15:16
Ye have not chosen me, but I have chosen you, and ordained you, that ye should go and bring forth fruit, and that your fruit should remain: that whatsoever ye shall ask of the Father in my name, he may give it you.

I have called you forth for this time and chosen you for My work. You will not be alone in your efforts. I am rallying others who will be a vital part of the strategy that will be released. I will teach you how to handle the increase. I will show you how to keep the flow and how to be My distributor, says the Lord. I have allowed you to be purified by fire and tested so that My Word will be the only thing left. Now, the desire to impress is gone. Now, the desire for your showing has been purged. Now, you only desire what I desire. I never wanted to see you hurt to this degree, but that will fade so quickly as you move into My purposes. Already it is going. I always know what is best and I move accordingly. You are a Joseph and others who will come along beside you will also be called Joseph. I am going to give you access that will enrich both you and others. There will be so much abundance and resource all around you that you will not be moved by it; you will only be moved by Me, says the Lord. I love you and I look forward to what is about to happen. I sing and rejoice over you in this hour, my favored one, for the time to favor you has come, says the Lord!

Prayer:
Lord,
You are the God of Endless Supply. Give me wisdom and Kingdom strategies to bring forth abundant resources in the Body of Christ.
In Jesus' Name,
Amen

Personal Check Points:

_____

_____

_____

_____

_____

_____

_____

Encounter 3

Formed For My Glory

Isaiah 43:7
Even every one that is called by my name: for I have created him for my glory, I have formed him; yea, I have made him.

I am forming you for My Glory. I have pressed and I have lingered. You are being shaped and formed in My hand. I have placed My hand on these places in your life to prepare you for what I have ordained. It has taken this path to cause you to understand My call. My child, I have not withheld from you. I have had you in a place of constant and intense gazing. I have penetrated the darkness in your behalf. I have gone before you to cause the confusion to stop. Your former shape could not contain My intentions for you. I am causing you to know this now. Allow Me to do My work. Leave these situations to Me. Your position now is to yield. I have remade you many times. Now, what I am forming will be lasting, says the Lord, and you will be set upon a focus of effectiveness in Me. So worship before Me and let Me heal what has been mishandled by others. For I, alone, am your maker and I do form you for My Glory, says the Lord!

Prayer:

Lord,
I am like clay in the Potter's Hand. Help me to yield to Your process of formation.

In Jesus' Name,
Amen

Personal Check Points:

_____

_____

_____

_____

_____

_____

Encounter 4

Stirring You For Change

Deuteronomy 31:8
And the LORD, he it is that doth go before thee; he will be with thee, he will not fail thee, neither forsake thee: fear not, neither be dismayed.

I am stirring your spirit for change. I am coming to you with change, says the Lord. Do not fear for I will strengthen you and help you. I will even hold you up with My hand. I consider this My responsibility. Let Me hold you up in this season of aloneness in Me. This will be our time of commitment together in this process. Even though you have been hungry for My will, the things that I am about to do, you have not asked for. They are in My plan and in My will. They are more glorious than you can imagine. I am going to heap upon you the rewards of faithfulness. I am going to give you a Divine Confidence that will transcend all the fear. Move and I will move with you, says the Lord. This is My time of acceleration and accomplishments in the Spirit.

Prayer:
Lord,
Changes are on the way. Thank You for your strength and help as You hold me up in each new season of change.
In Jesus' Name,
Amen

Personal Check Points:

_____
_____
_____
_____
_____
_____
_____

Encounter 5

The Current Press

Psalms 38:9
Lord, all my desire is before thee; and my groaning is not hid from thee.

This press is of My Spirit says the Lord. I must work within in order to manifest what I will do outwardly. I have laid upon you what is called the burden of the Lord. I long and I cry. Express what is within. Come before Me and release the groaning of your spirit. Step aside from the mindsets of those who would distract and find the place in Me that will bring fruition. Do what is necessary. Wail before Me. For that which I have ordained shall be known at this time. What you are looking for is in Me. What you long for is in Me, says the Lord. You will find fulfillment in Me. This process of separation unto this call and this season must be completed. Lay your fears before Me and tell me openly of your love and obedience unto Me. I want your heart - all of it, says the Lord. I will fill you with passion for My will in a refreshed zeal and you shall come forth with a new authority and a new countenance will witness that you have been with Me, says the Lord.

Prayer:
**Lord,
Your heart is crying to come forth.
Give me a new passion to capture your heart.
In Jesus' Name,
Amen**

Personal Check Points:

_____

_____

_____

_____

_____

_____

Encounter 6

Increased Strength

Psalms 18:32
It is God that girdeth me with strength, and maketh my way perfect.

I am your eternal strength. I am the source of strength and abiding joy. I am your quietness and I am your confidence. I am your authority and I am your guide. If I stand for you, who can be against you? This redefining is necessary for your next stage of development. This is a time of increased strength. The fortitude that will come forth will be a foundation for the maturity of others around you. This is not for you alone, but for others that I have called unto you. For as you come up unto a higher place in Me, others must come in order to partake of your visionary experience. Be prepared for promotion as you make the steps upward carrying My authority, for I have positioned you, says the Lord, and you shall overcome as you hold up the authority of the Lord!

Prayer:

**Lord,
You are the strength of my life. I ask for Your wisdom to strengthen others.
In Jesus' Name,
Amen**

Personal Check Points:

_____

_____

_____

_____

_____

_____

Encounter 7

You Will Be Brought Forth

Isaiah 43:2
When thou passeth through the waters, I will be with thee; and through the rivers, they shall not overflow thee: when thou walkest through the fire, thou shalt not be burned; neither shall the flame kindle upon thee.

I am bringing you through, says the Lord. Together we will accomplish this task. I did not set you upon a course of failure. I set you up to understand more of My ways. Man does not know this. This only comes from the School of My Spirit, says the Lord. You have wanted so many times to abandon this, but knew that you could not let go of the vision that I placed within. Your sufferings are going to produce the fruit of understanding and peace. Be at peace now, My Child. I have called you to Peace. From this moment, you will no longer struggle with My authority, but you will rest in Me in a repose of spirit that has alluded you for many days. Know that I am on board, and what I have started, I will accomplish, says the Lord!

Prayer:
Lord,
You are the Way-Maker. Give me Your peace as I continue on my journey.

In Jesus' Name,
Amen

Personal Check Points:

_____

_____

_____

_____

_____

_____

Encounter 8

Purged To Strengthen

II Timothy 2:20-21
But in a great house there are not only vessels of gold and of silver, but also of wood and of earth; and some to honour, and some to dishonour. If a man therefore purge himself from these, he shall be a vessel unto honour, sanctified, and meet for the master's use, and prepared unto every good work.

Do not fear the face of man, says the Lord, for I am with you. Even though you have been long patient, now I am requiring you to move. If you will delay any longer, YOU will be the one that displeases Me. The purging will not be for your damage, but it will be to strengthen. For if you do not move quickly, says the Lord, there will be, as it were, an infection that will rage throughout the Body. Your words and course of action will be the catalyst of change, says the Spirit. For as you do, My healing and strength shall be restored unto you and you will find the power to leap over the things that have stood before you. You have in your heart the very thing that needs to be done, now step out in obedience and do all that I have put in your heart, for I am going to release the weights, saith the Lord!

Prayer:
**Lord,
You are the True Vine of stability.
Help me to realize more and more
Your words - "For without Me you
can do nothing."
In Jesus' Name,
Amen**

Personal Check Points:

_____

_____

_____

_____

_____

_____

Encounter 9

Set In Order That Which Lacks

Proverbs 16:3
Commit thy works unto the LORD, and thy thoughts shall be established.

I have somewhat against you, says the Lord, but I have not left you alone. You are about My business and I know the inward thoughts of your heart, but you must take time to set in order that which is lacking. I will not allow the acceleration until My order is restored. I can do this with your help, says the Lord. Begin to cooperate with Me and the things that are already in your heart, for I have placed them there, says the Lord. Move forward in confidence. When you move forth, know that I have already prepared the way and gone before you. If you could see what I have, you would not hesitate. But I call upon you to use your faith now and to go for that which you do not see, for it will surely manifest, says the Lord. I will teach you to trust me completely. You are going to see that My way is perfect and that I have plans for you that are wonderful beyond your imaginations. Let this Word grip your spirit and obey Me in joy, for I will work and you will see My Glory, says the Lord.

Prayer:

**Lord,
Your thoughts toward me are more than can be numbered. Feed me with Your Word and Spirit that I may comprehend Your plan.
In Jesus' Name,
Amen**

Personal Check Points:

_____

_____

_____

_____

_____

_____

_____

Encounter 10

I Am Not Moved By This Storm

Isaiah 4:6
And there shall be a tabernacle for a shadow in the daytime from the heat, and for a place of refuge, and for a covert from storm and from rain.

I am not moved by this storm, says the Lord. Remain subject unto Me, ever listening for My voice. I will come to you. If I did not allow this, I would stop it right now, but it is not time. I am still in control. You must learn to follow Me in spite of the circumstances and you must learn to never, ever take your eyes off Me. There is nothing to hard for Me and there is no storm that

I do not stand over as Master and Lord! Nothing is greater than the Power of My Word. Do not be terrorized and fretful. Do not be moved for soon you shall be supernaturally carried and this storm shall cease, says the Lord!

Prayer:
Lord,
Your eyes are ever upon me. Comfort me with your strong arm and gentle voice.

In Jesus' Name,
Amen

Personal Check Points:

_____

_____

_____

_____

_____

_____

_____

Encounter 11

Tell Me Of Your Hunger

Psalms 107:9
For he satisfieth the longing soul, and filleth the hungry soul with goodness.

I am calling you to Me. You have seen so much and, yet, you are dissatisfied. You cannot find Me in the busy place. You must withdraw to tell Me of your hunger. Never have I let you down. But I will let you see enough emptiness that you have no other place to turn but unto Me. I am bringing a new dimension into your ministry. I am causing you to wait before Me and to see the invisible. You will see it, says the Lord, and then you will declare it. For what you have failed to accomplish, I will now show you My method, and I will do it, says the Lord. I am doing a new thing and it will be seen by many. Do not hold back and do not fear; do not even think of anything or anybody other than Me, says the Lord. Let Me consume you and I will consume your ministry. The fear of the Lord shall return.

What you bless, I shall bless; and what you curse, I will curse. You must understand the reverence of My move. Do not be frivolous. Be intent on seeing Me and I will show up, says the Lord. You will be amazed at My sweeping power and your spirit will be caught up as in a waterspout, says the Lord and you will not even see the people, but only My glory, says the Lord!

Prayer:

Lord,
You are the Lover of my soul. Fill me with a consuming passion for Your heart.

In Jesus' Name,
Amen

Personal Check Points:

_____
_____
_____
_____
_____
_____

Encounter 12

Clothed With Me

Isaiah 54:17
No weapon that is formed against thee shall prosper; and every tongue that shall rise against thee in judgement thou shalt condemn. This is the heritage of the servants of the LORD, and their righteousness is of me, saith the LORD.

I am going to clothe you with Myself, says the Lord. You will be shielded and walk right in the midst of the arrows, but they will be deflected. In the past, your soul has not been protected because you received the words that had been spoken. I am going to give you wisdom in these circumstances, says the Lord. I call you to walk above the flesh and to run into Me in the time of storm. Do not panic in your heart, says the Lord, for I am causing you to focus entirely by faith in

Me, and not to walk by sight. I am working in your behalf and I am causing new seeds of birth to come into your life. More than anything else, I am forming My nature in you, even in the midst of these difficulties. Expansion is coming and a new strength, says the Lord!

Prayer:
**Lord,
You are the God of All Might. Help me to know that no weapon formed against me will prosper.
In Jesus' Name,
Amen**

Personal Check Points:

_____
_____
_____
_____
_____
_____

Encounter 13

The Weight Of Your Heart

Proverbs 5:21
For the ways of man are before the eyes of the LORD, and he pondereth all his goings.

Do not be discouraged, My child. I have felt the weight of your heart and am holding you in My hand. It is time for a change in your methods of leadership and I am calling for a response from you at this time. You cannot bear this alone. I am raising up a people. Some will be in your midst, others will come in. Go find those that I have joined to you. Search them out, for they will be found in various places. I have assigned special ones to you. Look for My appointments. Do not stay in the cave, says the Lord, but come forth and go out. I call you to sacrifice in this. You have stayed in too close, says the Lord. Reach into the borders beyond, and you will find precious ones who will help. I am with you and I am at work as I build My many-membered Body, says the Lord!

Prayer:

Lord,
Your eyes are ever searching. Join my heart to those that You have ordained in my life.
In Jesus' Name,
Amen

Personal Check Points:

_____

_____

_____

_____

_____

_____

_____

Encounter 14

Bring Forth The Acceleration

Isaiah 48:6
Thou hast heard, see all this; and will not ye declare it? I have shown thee new things from this time, even hidden things, and thou dids't not know them.

I am moving you into a new season, says the Lord. I have something in mind, says the Lord, that will bring forth acceleration into what I have ordained for you. This is not what man has ordained, or even wanted, but it is what I want says the Lord, and it is what will be. I will not be bound by the mindsets of men; I will not confine your ministry to the imprisonment of religious attitudes, says the Lord. I free you, My called one; I free you from those who do not know the shift that I am taking you through. I have called you and I have ordained you so do not limit Me; Follow Me now and begin to move into this new thing, says the Lord. Do not look back, and do not go back. I have commanded a blessing in My new move, says the Lord your God, and that is where you will find the fulfillment. Old paths will not fulfill you now and old mindsets will no longer appeal to you; for what I do now shall be a formation of new things and new ways, and new mindsets. Step out in faith and do not worry about the resources, says the Lord, for an apostolic anointing to receive shall come upon you and you shall see a hunger in those that I have called and joined to you. It shall come forth, says the Lord!

Prayer:

> **Lord,**
> **You are the Model Apostle. Shift me into a mindset of apostolic reformation.**
>
> > **In Jesus' Name,**
> > **Amen**

Personal Check Points:

_____

_____

_____

_____

_____

_____

Encounter 15

Called To Write

Revelation 1:19
Write the things which thou hast seen, and the things which are, and the things which shall be hereafter;

I have called you to write, says the Lord. This is a day of My revealing. Your tongue has become the pen of a ready writer. I have held you in My arms in an humble position of learning. Now, take the ink and hurl it against the powers of darkness that have held my people in bondage for lack of knowledge. I will provide the way; but first, you must be diligent. You have been at the point of low confidence in this, but I am restoring hope to you in this matter, says the Lord. You will feel the press of My Spirit. You must obey

- - you must! My future plans for you depend upon your obedience at this level. Trust Me now, as I am working a timetable for you. I know all and see ahead of you, My child. As you move in obedience, a new sphere of influence will be opened unto you, and the labor of confident obedience shall be rewarded, says the Lord.

Prayer:
**Lord,
You are the Author of our faith. As You have called me, enable me to remain faithful.
In Jesus' Name,
Amen**

Personal Check Points:

_____

_____

_____

_____

_____

_____

Encounter 16

Declare What I Have Given

Deuteronomy 1:21
Behold, the LORD thy God hath set the land before thee: go up and possess it, as the Lord God of thy fathers hath said unto thee; fear not, neither be discouraged.

The heavens declare My glory, says the Lord, and even shall you declare what I have given. Now is the time of release. That which has been held in reserve in your spirit, must now come forth. This shall come forth as a sound from the heavens. It shall come as a sound throughout the region, for now is My time. You have contemplated, but now is the time for action. I give you new territory, says the Lord, so arise to possess it. Do not be held back for lack of resources, for I will provide as you go. Each new step will open new deposits of My provision. Refuse to die the slow death of indecision. Arise to assemble the people, for there are those that are called unto this vision. Be bold and release what I have placed within. The resources will be there. I shall go with thee, and it shall be even as I have spoken, says the Lord!

Prayer:

**Lord,
You are the Lion that roars. Possess my voice so that I may arise and release Your voice to the people that are sent to hear.
In Jesus' Name,
Amen**

Personal Check Points:

_____

_____

_____

_____

_____

_____

Encounter 17

Enlargement

Psalms 143:10
Teach me to do thy will; for thou art my God: thy Spirit is good; lead me into the land of uprightness.

I am leading you into new realms, says the Lord. There are new opportunities. I tell you to take a risk in faith! The security of what you have known will be no more, for now you must stretch forth and you will be so stretched that you will never again fit into the former. This is my doing, says the Lord. I am bringing enlargement, but it will not be easy to your flesh. What you sense now in your spirit, is the witness of the agony of the separations that you must walk in so that you may fulfill my will. This is a time of death, as well as life. You must release all to me - - all failures and all successes. If you release, I will. I am requiring you to walk before Me in faith. Know My voice and move forward at the sound of My call. I am already here; I await you now. The future is unknown only to you - - I am already here. I am forever present. Look ahead and move on for this is the day of fulfillment of all things, says the Lord.

Prayer:
    Lord,
    You are my Ultimate Security. Thank You for constantly being there on my way to fulfillment of destiny.
        In Jesus' Name,
        Amen

Personal Check Points:

_____

_____

_____

_____

_____

_____

_____

Encounter 18

Release Of Resources

Exodus 20:3
Thou shalt have no other gods before me.

I am grieved when My people disobey and dishonor Me, says the Lord. At this season, I call for release. I call for a release of resources such as has never been. My people shall have no other gods beside Me. I AM OWNER, says the Lord; I will not be bound by those who would seek to tie My hands. I AM about to open and pour! Make ready for My provision, says the Lord. Step out in faith - - NOW IS THE TIME. This is a time of loosening whatever I have need of. The money is about to be loosed says the Lord! Do not look to the promises of others, but LOOK UNTO ME and there will be a performance of what I have showed you, says the Lord.

Prayer:
**Lord,
You are the Possessor of my life and the Provider of all my needs. Thank You for an immediate release of finance and resources.
In Jesus' Name,
Amen**

Personal Check Points:

_____

_____

_____

_____

_____

_____

_____

Encounter 19

Spirit Of Confidence

Proverbs 14:26
In the fear of the LORD is strong confidence: and his children shall have a place of refuge.

I am bringing you to a new place of security in Me, says the Lord. You will no longer battle from a position of uncertainty and weakness. But as you find your place in Me, says the Lord, I will allow you to experience the Rock of My Presence as you have never before. None of these things will move you. Come up in Me and know Me. There will be security in Me, says the Lord. You must spend more time in My Presence. A spirit of confidence will come from the relationship that we have and the confidence that you develop in Who I AM to you! Have not I given you all things already? Have not I already paid the price? Have not I already told you of My plans for you? Have not I moved for you in the past when all hope was gone? Believe Me now with confidence, for I am aware and I AM here, says the Lord.

Prayer:
Lord,
Your Presence is everywhere. Cleanse me of all unbelief so that I may arise with a new confidence in the "I AM" that You are!
In Jesus' Name,
Amen

Personal Check Points:

_____
_____
_____
_____
_____
_____
_____

Encounter 20

There Must Be A Severing

Isaiah 46:10
Declaring the end from the beginning, and from the ancient times the things that are not yet done, saying, My counsel shall stand, and I will do all my pleasure:

I am calling you to go on. There are some things that must be severed and some that must be added. Some of this will happen as part of this process, and you will not have to be directly involved. You will be a part of other things. It is time to move into My vision for the House. No longer will you be bound by other's expectations, but you will move to meet Me, says the Lord. Deal with this in a different way for relationships change, says the Lord. Let My processes take effect. Allow it to happen. The move will bring My favor and the heavens will be open unto you. No longer will you be held back by the invisible shields that have been over you. But you will approach Me in clarity. You will hear Me in clarity, and you will have the confidence of knowing My will. This is not haughtiness, says the Lord, but overwhelming confidence that you know Me and that you have heard My voice. So now, follow, says the Lord and I will be with you!

Prayer:
**Lord,
You know the end from the beginning. Wrap me in the Confidence of Your Spirit.
In Jesus' Name,
Amen**

Personal Check Points:

_____

_____

_____

_____

_____

_____

Encounter 21

The Reformation

Acts 4:31
And when they had prayed, the place was shaken where they were assembled together; and they were all filled with the Holy Ghost, and they spake the word of God with boldness.

I am moving on you and through you. The changes that I am dropping into your spirit are of Me, and you will be bold to move forward. You can no longer follow those who are lagging behind. You must go on before others will move. You have been tempted to leave, but I say change. I say change, says the Lord. Bring the reformation of My plan. Start a revolution, and move forward. Do not die with the system, and do not give in. I call you to bring radical change through My processes. Open the door, even if you have to kick it down, says the Lord. I have not called you to be like them. I have called you to bring a challenge, and to maximize the potential of My people. Make a demand, says the Lord, in the realm of the Spirit. Stand in authority, and make the transition into the revolution. Watch the atmosphere change, says the Lord!

Prayer:

**Lord,
You stand in unequaled authority.
Maximize Your revolutionary power
in my life.
In Jesus' Name,
Amen**

Personal Check Points:

_____

_____

_____

_____

_____

_____

Encounter 22

Re-Define And Re-Evaluate

Isaiah 40:31
But they that wait upon the LORD shall renew their strength; they shall mount up with wings as eagles; they shall run, and not be weary; and they shall walk, and not faint.

I am calling you to redefine and re-evaluate relationships, saith the Lord. Even as I disclose problem areas and potential downfalls, now is the time to move with determined action designed to bring Me absolute glory. The Ministry that I have given has been only in the smallest of effects thus far. I have given you time to see the origin and the growth, so that you will know how to deal with additional areas that before you did not even know existed. I will take the load off. I will take the pressure off. Now is the time to get the Body in shape for the final run! This is vital that you run without hindrance! Now….cast aside the weights! Get ready for renewed vigor as you stand in obedience to My will, says the Lord, for the increase is at hand!

Prayer:

**Lord,
You see even the snares of the enemy. Protect me as I set my life for absolute obedience to Your will.
In Jesus' Name,
Amen**

Personal Check Points:

_____

_____

_____

_____

_____

_____

_____

Encounter 23

Beyond The Position of Predictability

Psalms 9:10
And they that know thy name will put their trust in thee: for thou, LORD, hast not forsaken them that seek thee.

I have not forsaken you, says the Lord, but am looking upon you with expectation. I am searching your heart. For it is in this season that your desire will come before Me. Do you want Me above all? Are you ready to take My yoke upon you, instead of the yokes of others? This is a time of release. When you are truly dead to acclamations, then I can move ahead for My utmost purpose and Glory. I am teaching you new ways, saith the Lord, and you are learning new things, even a new language. You have been in the position of predictability, now I move you beyond. Fear not to believe Me again for My will and My purpose. Flow with this press, and I will come forth, says the Lord, for I have ordained you for My purposes before the foundation of the world!

Prayer:

**Lord,
You are new every morning. Position me to receive new things in Your Presence.**

**In Jesus' Name,
Amen**

Personal Check Points:

_____

_____

_____

_____

_____

_____

_____

Encounter 24

You Will Have A Plan

Jeremiah 29:11
For I know the thoughts that I think toward you, saith the LORD, thoughts of peace, and not of evil, to give you an expected end.

I am going to give you a plan, says the Lord. You have been distraught far too long. Now, it is time to move in obedience. I am rising in this day to bring forth the completion of My plan of the ages. You must understand that what I am about to do, involves far more than you. But you must obey in order to be a part of My total plan. You do not understand the magnitude of this, because it has not been time to reveal it. This is why you must obey Me at every stage. The time is urgent, and I am moving swiftly. You have had enough time to trust me. You have developed enough to know that I am at work, and that I choose to use you. You do not need further confirmations. This is it, says the Lord. This is the Word that you have longed for. Now, allow me to thrust you forth by the power of My Spirit. This is the season of change. I am flowing now, but only in measure. If you commit to Me, I will take care of the issues that concern you. As you have desired a fuller measure of My anointing, so have I desired a fuller measure of commitment to walk in obedience to My Spirit. Give Me your fears, and keep your eyes upon Me for I will bring forth My submitted ones in this season, says the Lord.

Prayer:

Lord,
Your plans are so vast. Help me to forever keep my eyes on You.
In Jesus' Name,
Amen

Personal Check Points:

_____
_____
_____
_____
_____
_____
_____

Encounter 25

I Am Moving You

Amos 4:12
Therefore thus will I do unto thee, O Israel: and because I will do this unto thee, prepare to meet thy God, O Israel.

It is vital that I move you, says the Lord. I have not planned on stagnation in your life. Remember, I am the Author of the new birth. I am going to give you, as it were, a new birth. You will no longer have an excuse. This is My plan to move you to your destiny. I have begun this work in you, and I will complete it. My ways are perfect, and I am positioning you for even those things that you have not known. You have known Me, but you do not yet know the many birthings that I have for you. This is another stage. This is another realm. Do not be afraid of the unknown, for as long as you know Me, you will have everything you need. Your spirit has reached for Me, only to feel as if you did not find Me in fullness. I am going to show you how to cooperate with Me and to find what you are looking for. Only when the veil is removed, can you see Me. I am about to remove the veil, says the Lord, and you are about to behold Me and to come into the secret place of the Most High. There will I meet with you and when you come forth, you will have the confidence that you need for the next move in your life, says the Lord. Wait upon Me, and I will come.

Prayer:
**Lord,
You can even move Kings and Kingdoms. Help me to see You and You alone!**

     **In Jesus' Name,
     Amen**

Personal Check Points:

_____

_____

_____

_____

_____

_____

Encounter 26

You Are In My Hand

Psalms 91:1
He that dwelleth in the secret place of the most High shall abide under the shadow of the Almighty.

I will keep you in the palm of My hand, says the Lord. You have not moved from My Presence, and I am preparing you for what is yet to come. Every step has led you closer to accomplish My purposes, which are yet to unfold. Shut out the distractions so that you may hear My voice. I have not changed, and My Word is still the same. My directions and My purposes will still stand. All you need is confidence, which shall be built in the coming days. I am forming the iron of my will in your being. You will be stronger, and you will emerge with supernatural strength, says the Lord. I am going to allow victory to burst forth in the days ahead, and your faith will be encouraged. There will be a putting back and a restoration within your heart, for I am determined to bless and strengthen you, says the Lord!

Prayer:

**Lord,
Our pictures are engraven in the palm of Your hand. Thank you for continually restoring my life.
In Jesus' Name,
Amen**

Personal Check Points:

_____

_____

_____

_____

_____

_____

_____

Encounter 27

I Take Responsibility

Psalms 62:5
My soul, wait thou only upon God; for my expectation is from him.

I, alone, have called you. I am responsible for you. I will keep you, and I will direct you. Your next wave will be accompanied by the weapons of warfare that have been reserved for this hour. You have been worn out by moving in man's wisdom. I am pouring out My Spirit of Wisdom that will assure your victory, for by wisdom you shall make your warfare. Be still before Me and let My wisdom come forth. There is no reason to be afraid. Do not move until I tell you. When I give the Word, I will give the faith and the strength.

You will know what to do, but you must wait. My promises manifest to those who wait before Me. I am shaking everything that is not bound to you in the spirit. And I will loose you from strongholds, saith the Lord, for I am working on your behalf.

Prayer:

**Lord,
You are sufficient for every transition.
Help me to wait in Your Presence.
In Jesus' Name,
Amen**

Personal Check Points:

_____
_____
_____
_____
_____
_____
_____

Encounter 28

New Investments

Isaiah 33:6
And wisdom and knowledge shall be the stability of thy times, and strength of salvation: the fear of the LORD is his treasure.

I am calling you to make new investments. You have shared in times past the treasures of My deposits with those on certain levels, but now I am expecting more. There is another realm that I am bringing you into. This is a new venture between you and I, says the Lord. You will learn as you go. Do not delay due to the feelings of inferiority. Go beyond your fears and learn of Me in this new venture. Do not be afraid of mistakes. I will be with you. I will lay out before you opportunities for expansion. You shall have favor. Seek Me with all your heart, and be careful to return all glory and honor unto Me. I am getting ready to set you above, but remember the high place can be dangerous. You do not have to worry as long as you keep your eyes on Me and your motivation is to offer glory unto Me. I have purified your motives in many areas, says the Lord, but I will bring yet another test with this realm. Stay humble before Me, for I am bringing promotion, says the Lord.

Prayer:
Lord,
You are all wise. Help me to discern Your will in spiritual expansion.
In Jesus' Name,
Amen

Personal Check Points:

_____

_____

_____

_____

_____

_____

_____

Encounter 29

New Seasons

Isaiah 46:10
Declaring the end from the beginning, and from ancient times the things that are not yet done, saying, My counsel shall stand, and I will do all my pleasure.

I am calling you to progress further. You have come this far, but now it is time to travel again. Pick up your things, and get ready for the journey. If you do not do this now, you will not be ready at the appointed time. This is your final preparation call. It is not up to you to answer the questions that others may have. It is up to you to obey My Word! My purpose for you has not changed, but My season is even now changing. You have said to Me that you do not know what to do or how to do it; I will teach you. I have mentored you in the past, and I remain your Mentor. What I need from you is a heart of willingness and obedience. I am looking for fruits in your garden. When I see what I need to see, and I reach, taste and know that it has come into fruition, then I will unfold the signs and wonders that you have desired. But first, YOU must be ready. Work with Me, and watch in anticipation as to what I will do. I am moving quickly, so get ready, says the Lord!

Prayer:
**Lord,
You know the end from the beginning. Teach me the ways of Your Spirit so that I may move with You.
In Jesus' Name,
Amen**

Personal Check Points:

_____

_____

_____

_____

_____

_____

_____

Encounter 30

A Hearing Heart

Psalms 85:8
I will hear what God the LORD will speak: for he will speak peace unto his people, and to his saints: but let them not turn again to folly.

I have not left you without a word. I am giving you a hearing heart. There is a depth to understand, not only the words I speak, but the attitude of My heart. I am bringing you to an awareness of knowing Me. This will supersede what you have known of Me in the past. I will teach you by My Spirit. You are growing. I will now deal with you differently. You will know another realm of communion with Me. I will not only speak to you by the "hearing ear", but also by the "hearing heart". Get ready for a more powerful demonstration of My Spirit. Your level of faith is increased and I will help you to move out more quickly than you have in the past. Because you know Me more fully now, your confidence in Me will quickly be enlarged. Get ready for everything to change, says the Lord!

Prayer:

**Lord,
Your voice gives life. Prepare my heart for communion with You.
In Jesus Name,
Amen**

Personal Check Points:

_____

_____

_____

_____

_____

_____

_____

Encounter 31

The School Of Humility

Proverbs 22:4
By humility and the fear of the LORD are riches, and honor, and life.

I am bringing you to a new level of warfare. You will not strive in the flesh and exert your energies as you have in the past. This is a time for learning of Me. You will experience the training of My yoke, as I have never allowed it to be placed. Do not be drawn into situations that will not comply with My school of humility. Remember, I am far too wise to make a mistake. The present fires will burn out the will to stand in your flesh and to declare your glory; instead, you will bow before Me in the secret place and speak of My power, My might and My glory. There you will find a communion with Me that exceeds the fleeting glory of the performance expectations of people.

Be caught away with Me, and your ministry shall take a new perspective. Look for deliverance and vindication after your own obedience is fulfilled. Your assignment is now given, says the Lord, so go with the strength of My Mind. I will bring a closure to this quickly, for I confirm this to you even now, says the Lord, your Defender!

Prayer:

Lord,
You are the Supreme Example of Humility. Clothe me with the same spirit as I face each situation.
In Jesus' Name,
Amen

Personal Check Points:

_____

_____

_____

_____

_____

_____

_____

Encounter 32

I Have Already Heard

Psalms 28:6
Blessed be the LORD, because he hath heard the voice of my supplications.

I have already heard and marked to My heart the groanings from within and the anguish of your heart. I see and have been watching all along. I do confirm an end to the strife and the release of the ministry I have planted in your spirit. There is no need for Me to send someone to knock on your door with this message, for I have already given it. There is no need for your phone to ring, for I have already called you. Do not spend any more money looking for the word of confirmation concerning this. You have it already. The tension that you now experience will be swallowed up in the joy of surrender! I will not let you go, and I will not let you down, says the Lord. I am holding you tightly through this, and you will reap the fruits of your own labor, says the Lord, your Master.

Prayer:
**Lord,
You are a God who can speak ever so clearly. Thrust me into new surrenders for Your glory.
In Jesus' Name,
Amen**

Personal Check Points:

_____

_____

_____

_____

_____

_____

Encounter 33

A New Communion

Song Of Solomon 1:4
Draw me, we will run after thee: the King hath brought me into his chambers: we will be glad and rejoice in thee, we will remember thy love more than wine: the upright love thee.

You are now ready to enter into a new season of prayer. Your mind and thoughts are going to be quickened by My Spirit to enter into dialogue with Me. You will be quick to consult with Me and draw wisdom from My Mind. As you seek Me, you will never be ashamed. You are entering into a new reservoir of strength. You have gone so long on the giftings, now you must pursue the relationship. You must come into another season of knowing Me, says the Lord. Your strength in the day of battle will be weak if you do not follow the promptings of this new season of drawing. You need this now. I have timed this desire and this awakening for such an hour. Know that I will not fail thee, for your renewed strength is on its way and you will mount up with wings as an eagle, says the Lord!

Prayer:

**Lord,
You alone are life. Draw me and I will run after you.**

**In Jesus' Name,
Amen**

Personal Check Points:

_____

_____

_____

_____

_____

_____

Encounter 34

Arise In A New Mind

Isaiah 42:1
Behold my servant, whom I uphold; mine elect, in whom my soul delighteth; I have put my spirit upon him: he shall bring forth judgement to the Gentiles.

I am coming to you now. The things of the past must be repented of, and you must arise with new visionary leadership. Your lack in the past will not need to be carried over into this new dimension. You know where you have failed. Arise in a new mind, and move into the calling that I have for you. Cast aside the opinions of others, and move in what you are inclined to in your spirit. You have thought that such and such needed to be done - - I say to you that this is the prompting of My Spirit! Move now with the witness of My Spirit within! Many lives depend on what you do. You must cast aside the fears, and move forward in faith. You have been called and commissioned by My Spirit. I will validate My own Presence in My own way! Move, and I will move, says the Lord!

Prayer:

**Lord,
You have shown me what a
Leader should be. Grant me the
determination to move forward.
In Jesus' Name,
Amen**

Personal Check Points:

_____

_____

_____

_____

_____

_____

_____

Encounter 35

Refining Time

Zechariah 13:9
And I will bring the third part through the fire, and will refine them as silver is refined, and will try them as gold is tried: they shall call on my name, and I will hear them: I will say, It is my people: and they shall say, The LORD is my God.

I am molding you and bringing a refining. This process of purifying is essential to my plan and my next move among you. There are some who are not with you who must move on. There are others that I will bring in. Be open to Me and move slowly. I will accomplish My plan in My way. Let Me do My work and leave this to Me. I have waited until now so that you may be truly hungry for My will above all else. The time that has passed has been for you. You have needed a new alignment in your mind and in your emotions. Now this has come and it is time to bring a new element into the vision. Hold fast to My purposes and to My heart. Love Me with all your heart and you will see the dream come to pass, says the Lord.

Prayer:

**Lord,
You plant the desires of our hearts as we delight in You. Help me to hold fast to everything You have planted within my heart.
In Jesus' Name,
Amen**

Personal Check Points:

_____

_____

_____

_____

_____

_____

Encounter 36

A Place Of Letting Go

Jeremiah 46:27
But fear not thou, O my servant Jacob, and be not dismayed, O Israel: for, behold, I will save thee from afar off, and thy seed from the land of their captivity; and Jacob shall return, and be in rest and at ease, and none shall make him afraid.

I will cause a new thing to happen, says the Lord. I will bring you into a place of release, and you will rest in what I am about to do, even though you do not know. The peace shall pass your understanding, and you will be amazed at the rest in your spirit. For I am bringing you to a place of letting go, of confidence and security. The battle is really not yours at all. Your struggle is over. Call it over now. Call off the fight, and rest in Me. I am bringing into focus now much more than you have ever seen in the past, and it shall happen quickly. Just be and just do. Go about as I send you, and let the process of My Spirit come to fruition. Speak to yourself about this. Speak often and speak freely. Talk of what I am about to do. Say it out loud! Your ears will hear, and your own spirit will affirm that it is My voice, says the Lord. So say it out loud now, and feel the release of the power of your words over your own life and ministry, says the Lord your God!

Prayer:

Lord,
You are the God of Battles. Help me to rest in You until victory is manifested.

In Jesus' Name,
Amen

Personal Check Points:

_____

_____

_____

_____

_____

_____

_____

Encounter 37

Come Before Me And Receive Clarity

Ecclesiastes 7:8
Better is the end of a thing than the beginning thereof: and the patient in spirit is better than the proud in spirit.

I have called you, but you must be patient. You have tried to speak without hearing. First, you must hear. Then, you can speak. Do not be confused. Come before My Presence to receive the clarity that you need. I will tell you plainly. Discern My time. You have been through much pain because you have missed My perfect timing. Now, settle back into My Presence, and let Me be your Guide. All is not lost. You have learned from this error. You must first realize that it is your personal responsibility to hear My voice. If you have not tuned your ear properly to My Spirit, why do you blame others? Humble yourself, and take the responsibility. Do not explain to those who would question. Simply confess that you are seeking My face. I will meet with you, and when it is time, we will go out...together, says the Lord.

Prayer:
Lord,
You make the Secret Place a place of Holy Habitation. Help me to put aside every weight that would hinder our time together.
In Jesus' Name,
Amen

Personal Check Points:

_____

_____

_____

_____

_____

_____

Encounter 38

Let Me Reposition You

Proverbs 1:5
A wise man will hear, and will increase learning; and a man of understanding shall attain unto wise counsels:

Go back to prayer. Come before Me again, and let Me re-position you, says the Lord. I am not moved by other's expectations or even the trends of the day. I cannot grow what I have not birthed. Bring the ministry before Me so that My voice and My mind can permeate every area of service unto Me. There are things that must be changed. My mercy will be with you during this time as you bring all things unto My Lordship, says the Lord. I will speak clearly for I am a speaking

God, and I will make My voice clearly known unto you, says God. So arise in humility to obey the Voice of the Spirit that you have heard, for I am ready to bring fruition. The time is now! Hear now and move, says the Lord!

Prayer:

Lord,
You are the One who gives increase. Purge me from other's expectations so that I may bring forth fruit unto Your glory.

In Jesus' Name,
Amen

Personal Check Points:

_____

_____

_____

_____

_____

_____

Encounter 39

Changes .... NOW!

Daniel 2:21
And he changeth the times and the seasons: he removeth kings, and setteth up kings: he giveth wisdom unto the wise, and knowledge to them that know understanding.

I am bringing the changes now. The desire is being raised within you. The very thing that you have been questioning, you are now ready to embrace. Your longing for something more has come before Me as a cry for change. Your dissatisfaction has been used by Me to stir the changing of the seasons. I am bringing a change of seasons and a change of placements. You are about to step into a new arena of my workings, saith the Lord, and I am going to bring a release into your spirit. This release will bring a new mindset of raising up others. You have wanted so much to have approval. Now, seek My approval above all things. If you have My favor, all that you need will come, says the Lord. So go forward and be assured that My Word has come to you, even now, and I will cause you to become the head and not the tail, says the Lord!

Prayer:

**Lord,
Your timing is perfect. Cover me with Your favor as I step into a new arena of release in You.**

**In Jesus' Name,
Amen**

Personal Check Points:

_____

_____

_____

_____

_____

_____

_____

Encounter 40

Positioned For Choice

Deuteronomy 30:19
I call heaven and earth to record this day against you, that I have set before you life and death, blessing and cursing: therefore choose life, that both thou and thy seed may live:

I am positioning you for choice. What are you going to do? I stand back to watch and to observe your conduct in this time of choice. You have pondered this long enough; it is time now to take a stand. There is no need for further questioning when you already know what to do. I have led you in a plain path. Now is the time to put all indecision aside and move forward in faith. My will is a good will. My ways are perfect. I have no deception in My Will. When you move forward in faith, then you will know the joys of My anointing resting upon you in a greater measure, says the Lord. I have set the way before you. Now choose life, says the Lord, and you will release My Grace in this situation, says the Lord! Your Victory is here and it is in Me. I will not disappoint you in this matter, so be assured and go forward, for I will perform all that I have promised, says the Lord!

Prayer:
Lord,
Thank you for Your direction. Anoint me to move in the performance of Your perfect will.
In Jesus' Name,
Amen

Personal Check Points:

_____

_____

_____

_____

_____

_____

_____

Encounter 41

Old Methods Will Not Suffice

Isaiah 58:14
Then shalt thou delight thyself in the LORD; and I will cause thee to ride upon the high places of the earth, and feed thee with the heritage of Jacob thy father: for the mouth of the LORD hath spoken it.

I long to make your path easier. I have seen the struggles and have waited for this phase of your growth. Now that you are here, you must proceed with this new strategy. Old methods will not suffice for this level of advancement. I am changing the way that others view you. I am going to do this, even through your own obedience, coupled with My favor. Seek that you may excel in love and your advancement will be accelerated. I will teach you to respect what

I respect, so that you may imitate Me, says the Lord. There is coming a strength of position of meekness before Me that will give you the mantle of strength before others. Walk in this wisely, and you shall never lack, says the Lord of the Host of the Armies of Heaven!

Prayer:

**Lord,
Each time I move, You have gone before me. Cause me to move forward in the love of God.
In Jesus' Name,
Amen**

Personal Check Points:

_____
_____
_____
_____
_____
_____
_____

Encounter 42

You Are Getting Ready For Change

Jeremiah 29:11
For I know the thoughts that I think toward you, saith the LORD, thoughts of peace, and not of evil, to give you an expected end.

I have so much for you. You do not comprehend all that I am about to do. Move in faith. Trust Me for the outcome of the plans you are making! I move in ways that are incomprehensible to the mind of man. You are getting ready for a change. I am preparing you, and I am preparing those around you. It will only be but for a fleeting season more, then I shall move. You will see My evidence in all that I am doing. You will feel my Presence, and know that I am about to explode My will in your life. It is not My nature to remove even one thing that you really do need. And it is not My nature to give unto you that which you do not need, for I know what is just ahead. There are many things that you thought that you had to have, but those were not granted. Now you are beginning to understand why. Stay near to me, and you will hear exactly what I want you to know. Worship Me, and value highly what I place in your spirit.

Prayer:
**Lord,
Your plans are incomprehensible.
Help me to flow with change.
In Jesus' Name,
Amen**

Personal Check Points:

_____

_____

_____

_____

_____

_____

_____

Encounter 43

I Am Found In Solitude

Proverbs 8:17
I love them that love me; and those that seek me early shall find me.

You are entering a time of transformation. All that you will become is a result of all that has happened. I formed you through time. As the wind blew and the floods beat, you were being formed to meet My highest use. I have not wasted one thing in your life. When you continue to humble yourself before Me, you will know My will. I am not found in the wisdom of men. I am not found in the places that multitudes will seek. I am found in solitude. Remember, I passed through the crowd. You can find Me. Even though

I delight in hiding myself, I delight in making Myself known. You have earnestly prayed for My will. I will accomplish great and mighty things through you. As you position yourself for birth, I will do My part. You do your part, and trust Me with the rest. I am about to give you extra strength that will surpass and surprise you!

Prayer:

**Lord,
Draw me to a private place to meet with You. Thank You for choosing me.**

**In Jesus' Name,
Amen**

Personal Check Points:

_____
_____
_____
_____
_____
_____

Encounter 44

Qualified For This Will

Jeremiah 30:17
For I will restore health unto thee, and I will heal thee of thy wounds, saith the LORD; because they called thee an Outcast, saying, This is Zion, whom no man seeketh after.

You are being healed. There is a Ministry inside of you. Why do not you let Me manifest? Your injury has been larger to you than Me. Cast your gaze and sense of inability away from yourself. Your praise is being restored. Your worship will come before Me, and you will realize the pain is gone. Release all. You have been hanging around My perfect will. Now, go in. I qualify you. You will be baptized in boldness and love. I will effect a healing in your spirit, soul, and body that will cause My Life to bring you into My presence, and you will again minister to Me in pureness.

Prayer:
Lord,
You are the Healer of my spirit, my soul, and my body. Cleanse me and wash the wounds clean.
In Jesus' Name,
Amen

Personal Check Points:

_____
_____
_____
_____
_____
_____
_____

Encounter 45

Stand And Tell

II Chronicles 34:27
Because thine heart was tender, and thou didst humble thyself before God, when thou heardest his words against this place, and against the inhabitants thereof, and humbledst thyself before me, and didst rend thy clothes, and weep before me: I have even heard thee also, saith the LORD.

I am speaking more strongly to you now. Do not let this pass. You have overlooked what I have spoken. I long to rescue you from the pit. I have grieved over you. And even now I love you with a penetrating depth of affection. You have been called to minister unto Me and before Me. Your call is unto Me. When the waters of My Spirit start to flow, you will feel the swelling of the tides of My love, and I will draw you again. You have thought that this would not come, but it is here. It is here now. It is beginning, and you will respond. You have not turned your heart from Me. In all of your error, you have not turned from Me. I look upon the heart. Stand, and tell of your renewed love for Me. Let the cleansing come even in the face of those that have upheld you. Tell of this new relationship. Let the tears flow. Let your heart be expressed. My Spirit desires expression through you. Weep before Me, and show forth my praise in the midst of My people. For I will use you to stir up the love of the Bride for the Bridegroom.

Prayer:
> Lord,
> I am not ashamed of what You are doing in my life. Let my tears continuously bring You glory.
> In Jesus' Name,
> Amen

Personal Check Points:

_____

_____

_____

_____

_____

_____

Encounter 46

I Plan Ahead For You

John 10:27
My sheep hear my voice, and I know them, and they follow me:

Do not worry any longer. You have tried within yourself to make a way for this to happen, and it will not work. My next move for you is bigger than you think. I will move upon you and will set in motion that which is necessary for the vision. Right now, keep your ear attentive to My voice. There is a Word that I am speaking to you, and when you walk in total obedience, you will have the confidence that you need. I plan ahead for you for I know the Work that I have called you to do. The magnitude of My Works is so great that your present ministry is only a seed that will begin to change shape and form and will come forth and be transformed. You have shown Me that you are not a hireling. You have not served Me for mammon. I have trusted you with hardships and difficulty. Take heed, that you keep your heart pure before Me. Take heed, and stay before Me. Humble yourself continuously before My presence. For I am about to bless you and prosper you with a new level of finances. You have thought that your greatest test will be in prosperity. Prepare your heart now.

Humble yourself now. You are going to experience a breakthrough in your finances. Do not even think of how I am going to do it. Just follow Me and watch Me lead. You do everything that I say and I am here to guarantee a continual harvest. There is additional sowing that you must do for I am going to speak to you so that you may have the continual harvest. I am the Lord of the Harvest. Lay everything before Me. I am right on time. I embrace you now and tell you to not give up. You will see My Hand move shortly and My glory will cover you and you will melt before Me as I make a way and do the impossible, says the Lord.

Prayer: Lord,
I will fasten my eyes upon You as you lead. Cover me with Your eternal glory.

In Jesus' Name,
Amen

Personal Check Points:

_____

_____

_____

_____

_____

_____

Encounter 47

Anxious To Move For You

James 4:10
Humble yourselves in the sight of the Lord, and he shall lift you up.

I am anxious to move for you. As you follow My Word, I am going to relieve the pressure and stress. You have been considering what man wants, now consider what I want. Remember, My child, it is not what man expects out of you. Humble yourself before Me to do My will. I will help you make the adjustments. Remember, My Word gives you the requirements, but My Spirit gives the enablement. I will help you. You will not fail, and you will not be disappointed. Step out in faith, and do as I have commanded you. This is your hour of testing. If you do not move to obey My instructions now, do not expect the way to get easier for the way of a transgressor is hard. I have stretched Myself toward you, now go and do the work. I will support you with My hand. Come to Me for a cleansing, and then go forth to do what I have commanded for I am with you…. I uphold you….and I will give you the strength to continue.

Prayer:
Lord,
Your Word has spoken. Help me to make the necessary adjustments.
In Jesus' Name,
Amen

Personal Check Points:

_____

_____

_____

_____

_____

_____

Encounter 48

I Am Processing You

Isaiah 43:19
Behold, I will do a new thing; now it shall spring forth; shall ye not know it? I will even make a way in the wilderness, and rivers in the desert.

You are not alone. Even though you have been lonely, you are not alone. When I sent out my disciples, I did not send them out alone. I sent them out by two's. When I called the eight into the Ark, I provided for companionship. You are going to see My plan. Right at this moment, you are damaged. I wound, but I heal. There were lessons for you, My child, that had to come. Even now, I am processing you in this way for My Glory. You could not bear the glory that I am about to entrust you with without these lessons. It would destroy you as well as others. Your mind has become submissive to me. You are almost ready for the next level. The wisdom that you have attained in this way could not be found in the libraries of man. I allowed the furnace of affliction to burn away the dross of flesh that stinks so in My Presence. Until now, you have not been able to smell this stench of flesh. This has been such a repulsive smell to Me! I have held patience with you. Now, I am going to wrap you with a confidence of love. The cleansing is here and you will be renewed in the spirit of your mind. Old things are passed away, and behold, I make all things new! I will do a new thing. Get ready for excitement and anticipation to return!

Prayer:

Lord,
Thank you for revealing the glory of Your holiness and my own depravity. Help me to continuously be submissive.

In Jesus' Name,
Amen

Personal Check Points:

_____
_____
_____
_____
_____
_____

Encounter 49

Tune Your Ear To My Spirit

Matthew 11:15
He that hath ears to hear, let him hear.

I have called you, but you must be patient. You have tried to speak without hearing. First, you must hear. Then, you can speak. Don't be confused. Come before My Presence to receive the clarity that you need. I will tell you plainly. Discern My time. You have been through much pain because you have missed my perfect timing. Now, settle back into My Presence and let me be your Guide. All is not lost. You have learned from this error. You must first realize that it is your personal responsibility to hear my voice. If you have not tuned your ear properly to My Spirit, why do you blame others? Humble yourself and take the responsibility. Don't explain to those who would question. Simply confess that you are seeking My face. I will meet with you, and when it is time, we will go out together, says the Lord.

Prayer:

Lord,
My ears are open to hear Your Word.
Forgive me for failing to discern Your timing and Your voice.
In Jesus' Name,
Amen

Personal Check Points:

_____

_____

_____

_____

_____

_____

_____

Encounter 50

Say It Out Loud!

Psalms 81:10
I am the Lord thy God, which brought thee out of the land of Egypt open they mouth wide, and I will fill it.

I will cause a new thing to happen, says the Lord. I will bring you into a place of release and you will rest in what I am about to do, even though you do not know. The peace shall pass your understanding and you will be amazed at the rest in your spirit. For I am bringing you to a place of letting go, of confidence and security. The battle is really not yours at all. Your struggle is over. Call it over now. Call off the fight and rest in Me. I am bringing into focus now much more than you have ever seen in the past and it shall happen quickly. Just be and just do. Go about as I send you and let the process of My Spirit come to fruition. Speak to yourself about this. Speak often and speak freely. Talk of what I am about to do. Say it out loud! Your ears will hear and your own spirit will affirm that it is My voice, says the Lord. So say it out loud now and feel the release of the power of your words over your own life and ministry, says the Lord your God!

Prayer:
Lord,
 I offer my body, a living sacrifice. Fill my mouth with Your Words so that I may activate the atmosphere with the Power of the Living Word!
 In Jesus' Name,
 Amen

Personal Check Points:

_____
_____
_____
_____
_____
_____
_____

Encounter 51

Alignment Of Mind And Emotions

Luke 6:21
**Blessed are ye that hunger now: for ye shall be filled
Blessed are ye that weep now: for ye shall laugh.**

I am molding you and bringing a refining. This process of purifying is essential to My plan and My next move among you. There are some who are not with you who must move on. There are others that I will bring in. Be open to Me and move slowly. I will accomplish My plan in My way. Let Me do My work and leave this to Me. I have waited until now so that you may be truly hungry for My will above all else. The time that has passed has been for you. You have needed a new alignment in your mind and in your emotions. Now this has come and it is time to bring a new element into the vision. Hold fast to My purposes and to My heart. Love Me with all your heart and you will see the dream come to pass, says the Lord.

Prayer:
**Lord,
I submit my whole heart to Your leadership. Work Your work in Your way that You may receive all the glory.
In Jesus' Name,
Amen**

Personal Check Points:

_____
_____
_____
_____
_____
_____
_____

Encounter 52

A New Dimension

Jeremiah 35:15
I have sent also unto you all my servants the prophets, rising up early and sending them saying, Return ye now every man from his evil way, and amend your doings, and go not after other gods to serve them, and ye shall dwell in the land which I have given to you and to your fathers: but ye have not inclined your ear, nor hearkened unto me.

I am coming to you now. The things of the past must be repented of and you must arise with new visionary leadership. Your lack in the past will not need to be carried over into this new dimension. You know where you have failed. Arise in a new mind and move into the calling that I have for you. Cast aside the opinions of others and move in what you are inclined to in your spirit. You have thought that such and such needed to be done but I say to you that this is the prompting of My Spirit! Move now with the witness of My Spirit within! Many lives depend on what you do. You must cast aside the fears and move forward in faith. You have been called and commissioned by My Spirit. I will validate My own Presence in my own way! Move and I will move, says the Lord!

Prayer:
    Master and Lord,
    I know that you have prepared a new path for my feet. Teach me to move in Your perfect timing.
        In Jesus' Name,
        Amen

Personal Check Points:

_____

_____

_____

_____

_____

_____

_____

About The Author

Jana Alcorn is a humanitarian, author, strategist and Biblical motivator. She is an anointed servant of God who lives to express the heart of God to encourage all people from all walks of life. Through the Word and the Prophetic Anointing of the Holy Spirit, countless lives are being equipped, encouraged, empowered and evangelized. Her call to Love God, Lift People, and Launch Destinies is manifested throughout the nations. She has truly been called of God both apostolically and prophetically.

After a myriad of life's challenges, ranging from being kidnapped as a baby and then, most recently, her husband dying in her arms, she lives to do Kingdom work and to inspire others to overcome the difficult places of life. From the cotton fields of Alabama to the nations of the world, her passion is to propel others into their Divine destinies.

At the age of fifteen, her mother dropped her off at a bus station, where she traveled out of state to preach the Gospel for the very first time. Since that time, her ministry has taken her into almost thirty nations of the world. Her most current international project, Hayley's House - A House of Hope And Mentorship For Orphaned And Abandoned Children, an African orphanage, named for the Alcorn's daughter who was tragically killed in a car accident, is now a reality.

Jana received her education at various institutions including Snead State Community College, the University of Alabama, Southwestern University, Christian Bible College, Logos Bible Institute, Larson School of Real Estate and John Maxwell University. She currently holds her Doctorate in Biblical Studies.

www.JanaAlcorn.com

For the latest in news and ministry information from Jana Alcorn Ministries, please visit us online at:
www.JanaAlcorn.com.

Get up-to-date itinerary details as well as updates from all our Global Reach Ministries including:
- Dream Builders Network
- Dream Child Foundation
- Hayley's House
- H.O.P.E. *Helping Other People Elevate*

For your convenience and personal spiritual growth, be sure to shop our online store for the latest in resources.

> *Loving God,*
> *Lifting People,*
> *Launching Destinies*

Available at www.JanaAlcorn.com

Hope Speaks
Boldly Transform Your Life

Expectation is a key to receiving from God. Access the power of hope and boldly transform your life.

Hope Speaks and other books in this series are available at www.JanaAlcorn.com

Available at www.JanaAlcorn.com

Favor Speaks
Unlocking Your Potential

In this activating book, *Favor Speaks*, you will discover open doors to your Divine Connection. Unlock your favorable future!

Favor Speaks and other books in this series are available at www.JanaAlcorn.com

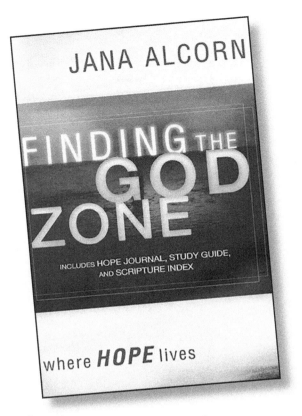

Finding the **GOD ZONE** *provides Hope in the midst of the chaos. Real life stories of lost expectation and hope restored are combined with biblical principles. The companion Study Guide, Journal, and Scripture Index provide resources that help you delve deeply into life's twists and turns with prayerful reflection enlightening revelation.*

Published by

AVAILABLE WHEREVER BOOKS ARE SOLD.

Connect with @JanaAlcorn on these social media sites for her latest

blurbs, blog and media....

- Updates
- Pictures
- Interaction
- Video
- Latest Blog
- Calendar

CPSIA information can be obtained
at www.ICGtesting.com
Printed in the USA
BVHW082230140220
572367BV00001B/7